A Kayak is My Church Pew

# A Kayak is My Church Pew

Poems by

Patricia Carney

Cover design by Shay Culligan
Cover photograph by Patricia Carney

ISBN: 978-1-952326-64-6

Kelsay Books
502 South 1040 East, A-119
American Fork, Utah, 84003

# Acknowledgments

My thanks to the Knowles-Nelson Conservation Program and the Conservation Board Members. This program makes land and water conservation possible, allowing for accumulation and preservation of thousands of acres of wilderness lands in Wisconsin and especially the area known as the Turtle-Flambeau Flowage.

Special thanks to Ken and Audrey Hart, the innkeepers at Cry of the Loon Resort. which provided excellent lodging each July for over 20 years so that my family and I could explore this body of water called, "The Crown Jewel of the North," by the Wisconsin Dept. of Natural Resources. Thanks to my husband, Bob Jursik, who frequently paddled with me, especially in the days we used our double kayak exploring Big Island, Four Mile Creek, Lake of the Falls, and Murray's Landing along with other remote areas of the flowage.

Special mention and thanks to the members of our poetry camp in May with instructor, Robin Chapman, at The Clearing in Door County who critiqued many of the poems in this collection.
My thanks also to Mike Kriesel, who helped edit this collection, and Cheryl Nenn, Riverkeeper in Milwaukee County, avid paddler and fellow member of the board, Preserve Our Parks, for encouraging my poetry.

Epigraph by Robert Frost in the first poem, "A Kayak is my Church Pew" is from A MASQUE OF MERCY, 1947, Published by Henry Holt and Company. This quote in full reads, *I say I'd rather be lost in the woods/Than found in church,* p.28, and is recited by a character named, Keeper.

# Contents

# A Kayak Is my Church Pew

*I'd rather be lost in the woods than found in church.*
—Robert Frost

From Flambeau shores, the baptismal waters
of my spiritual blessings, I observe all-in-all
light-in-light, hushed in calm stillness—witness
                                        creation once more.

Kayaking through this first garden of Genesis,
I find gilled creatures using summer warmth
to reproduce and fulfill prime law of formation:
                                        species regeneration.

In primordial pool, my paddle sends echoing rings
throughout dawn—passing first fishing camp, I bow
to an ancient totem in center: wood carved life cycle
                                        of predators over prey.

Bear stands tall, songbird on shoulder, and on top
of bear's head: A Great Bald Eagle, spirit soaring
with wings spread, wrapping whole earth in encasing
                                        embrace of his kingdom.

Life cycle depicted on totem is icon to God of creation—
our primal mystery, the All-Knowing, All-Present.
My paddle skims surface, forms new circling rings,
                                        surrounded by blessings.

# Turtle-Flambeau Flowage

*A flowage is a flowage,*
the old woman responded
to question on why she stayed
eighty years on a lake named, Crystal,
knowing I lodged at Turtle-Flambeau.

After reflecting, she continued:
*a flowage is really only a river*
*backed-up by a damn dam,*
*one that holds back the water*
*over granite rock and pristine forest.*

I considered her aged wisdom: Old-
growth trees stood for scores of decades,
roots finally overwhelmed, succumbed,
until felled, now driftwood, wind-
swept in backwater graveyard bays.

Damming the confluence of two rivers,
act of craven disregard for two watersheds,
dislodging plant and animal communities.
Nearly a century later, I now kayak this
flowage still finding bark-less driftwood

sun-bleached, windswept in graveyard bays,
yet new communities now thrive on different
miles and miles of shorelines around islands,
protected lands held a century in antiquity
of what these elders once called high-ground.

# Musky Skull

I paddled upon a bone white skull,
tissue, sinew, and guts picked clean,
maybe ants after otter musky meal.

Fisherman's great trophy fish, fierce
fighter, now mounted on river rock,
find of the day for tourist of a flowage.

Skeleton is left to fend-off elements,
unprotected, now unwanted, meat gone.
Bones speak to sturdiness of structure.

Left in dry place, musky bones last
years, chip down to gravel, then dust,
but never ashes flung over forest floor.

# Mother's Nursery Aerosol Freshener

Pond in far back, out-of-the-way, back bay
of expansive flowage, out of the current
and news of summer, visitors, and fishers.

Creatures, all raised in pond nursery amid
bloodsuckers, nymphs and minnows, all
swimming now in the flowing river water.

An earthy-mother smell is mired in muck
behind the tall pencil-thin brown cattails
amid the sludge of green algae and reeds.

Small ripples of tadpole flagellum move
pond eggs along in slow slimy stew baking
under the heat of mid-July at mid-day lull.

A lush green curtain pulled aside, opening
at a mid-pond round kitchen table set atop
with long logs on pond's surface gleaming

under full sol, giving flat porcelain counter-
top the sparkling surface of a silvery mirror.
This pond table is set with lovely water lilies

set on top thin green platters with blossoms
ringing pond's bosom in yellow flowery lei.
Such lush lily fragrance conceals old pond

scum odor like an aerosol freshener sprayed
to subdue the fishy smell of many amphibian
and reptilian babies teeming in pond nursery,

oozing from odors of the rotting decay while
nurturing the new life of flowage in mud soup
with salty scents amid fish oil drenched algae.

# Damselfly

dances under moon
to her demise

nymph in water
for a year or more

emerges to air
her sole fantasy

just a few weeks
to fulfill a flight

to mate and lay
eggs in a gel pack

on submerged
green reed

leaving young
in slipstream of life

her skeleton
submerged once more

# Kettle-Skull Safe

With thumb head and clawed feet
shaped like fried bacon protruding
from shell larger than a frying pan,
this turtle grabs a tiny grub to eat.

Hungry from winter hibernation
a snapping turtle eats whatever it
can get to its mouth, when satiated,
lays sunning upon a long floating log.

If a predatory otter nears, the turtle dives
to bottom withdrawing head and feet,
escaping into the safety of a kettle-skull
to rest upon river rocks, camouflaged,

while keeping soft undercarriage safely
wedged against rounded rocks to shore-
up a vulnerable core, a turtle's energy
of effort always spent in warding-off.

# Drone has Landed

Two short hops and shiny
metallic green biplane
comes to rest on long smooth
runway of my kayak bow,

a refueling rest stop mid-way
in shipping channel with
gunner tail propped on six legs.

Goggled head of pilot takes
bearings and when fully rested
will be ready for takeoff from
same runway of longbow.

I steadied the kayak for this
maneuver and leveled paddle
for readiness of flight mission:

Impregnate the many females
for recruitment of new armies
of nymphs to fill ranks of these
storied legions of dragonflies.

# Watchful Wait

Loon cry echoes
through morning fog

reverberating
over water

repeating waves
strike shoreline shallows

such hollow echo
nearly mournful

a call to his mate
sitting on reedy nest

reassuring her
of his watchful wait

her very egg
oval container

for this whole
echoing world.

# Leveraging Water

Paddlers seek calm waters,
shelter on the lee side of the isle,
yet nearby sailors were mad

caught in irons, handcuffed
by the stills, wanting an escape,
seeking the wind billowing

through sails, with bow
hard into the blow, tri-cornered
jib like inflated half balloon.

Admiring the art of wind skills,
kayaker witnesses behind the island
wall, passive, not fighting the flow,

for paddlers leverage the water
going with the wind, and returning
behind a lee shore, peacefully.

Wood ducks paddle all in a row.

# Summer Flats

When the summer altitude relaxes
at about 46 degrees north latitude
regressing to a pre-Copernican age,
summer flattens out to equal light-dark
days, a time between migration and
a great exodus, wildings having settled—
the task of the day: basking in the sun.

This lull of flat-earth balancing out at
the mid-point fulcrum of light's teeter-
totter, its length now long straight board,
not inclined between spring or fall equinox.
Little energy is expended keeping warm
while pelts shed with the sun over-head,
ripe berries and seeds there for the taking.

Box turtles with shells large as frying
pans climb onto round rocks protruding
from muddy flats of riverbed while the
dragonflies perch on their scored shells,
leaving damselflies to the green flats
of lily pads spreading-out over smooth
surface water behind some stagnant bend.

Too soon, flat days give way to eroding
of Beaufort four or more, stirring the waves.
Summer slants away from the flats with
light waning while new licking waves cover
over sandbanks washing away dry flats.
Light fades, exodus begins, day slants
into cold: basking gives way to surviving.

# Sanskrit on Sand

fossils embedded in rock
washed ashore
Sanskrit on sand

a Rosetta Stone
for reading genesis
of this riverbed

creatures and shells
trapped on ice shelves
centuries of creeping ice flow

short-lived but long recorded
entrapped impressed
fossilized 50,000 years ago

geologists carbon date
fossils from long past
sliding ever south

this long ago
slow march of time
of life gone in a flash—

flash forward to now:
what trace of splash
is this life now lived?

# Knotty Pine Novel

Sailors know the art of knots.
As a paddler, I collect this art,
not the sailor's kind, but real:

knots expelled from tree limbs
or stumps off broken branches.
I find them in sandy shallows,
cast-offs of flowage driftwood.

Trees may be seen as straight
and tall; they're not, they spiral,

rising and branching to balance
sprouting limbs side-to-side, then
quartering until a sprout hardens
around a cross-grained knot

as a ball and socket allowing legs
then arms to branch out from a trunk,
the knee knots and elbow knots
forming joints for limbs mid-way up.

My mother's wisdom: *What goes
around, comes around* taught about
what-not, knots contain the same story
of some family tree branching-out

captured in the grain of a round knot.
Just read a knotty-pine novel to
know the art of a branching knot.

# Reflections

I

kayak

a quiet kayak

in the backwaters

and bayous behind

the wind—still waters

more a mirror than lapping

lake reflecting the tall pines as

same boughs laid down. With this

reflection of an inner-eyed perception

confusing my finity with infinity

a minds-eye begged to

know where is the

center of it all?

Is it not the

kayak

and

I

# Granite Rock Protrudes

through the surface of flowage,
rock face before the dam(*n*)
now a lone island above,
marking archipelago below.

Long slender granite crack
serves as a footing for a jack
pine marking isle sounding
as if navigator's lighthouse.

One lone pine against a whole
forest of jack pines fencing
far shoreline, chart marking
pine for way-finding symbol.

Sure-handed paddler floating
near measures the long kayak
width as stone mason fudging
and humoring each new stone—

Maneuvering around the swells
rippling over sharp under-rocks
while balancing a long paddle,
just as a mason working for level.

Protruding rock is as singular
as the lone jack pine while sub-
merged rocks in shallows are
as plentiful as shoreline forest.

Keen kayaker peers deep below
the wind ripples to see pristine
traces here of what was created
once, long ago, before the flow.

# Mid-Day Lull

Floating on Flambeau Flowage
on a windless day, paddle still,
adrift at midstream,

mind adrift too—
*What's below?* World of scaled
and clad creatures, gills needed.

Cloudless day, full sun at noon.
*What's ashore?* Scurriers find
shade under hanging pines,

damp under-moss cool.
Fishermen inside too,
noon is siesta time.

Rare stillness, no wind
meaning no waves,
watery surface smooth,

skin-like sheath.
Maybe for one moment
I own this world,

a body of water all mine.
*What's above?*
That's for another day.

# Where Beavers Build Dams

Drifting in stills, the stagnant water
near wind pools after heavy rains,
I escape from the rushing current

pushed by wind and tons of water
confined within deep bank narrows,
all scrambling toward a torrent of falls
or roaring rapids over barrel boulders.

It is a calm separated from striving
hidden behind sand bars, tiny islets,
Eden behind smooth slipstream.

Creatures come for sabbatical here
to lay eggs and hide new broods
of downy chicks away from raptors.

The damselflies and dragonflies
deposit eggs for new water nymphs
while water striders skittle along as
beavers build dams, aiding the stills.

It is a resting breather, sun-drenched
wayside, before venturing again
into the rushing winds and currents,
and competition of predator vs. prey.

# A Convertible

Any kayak paddler
will wish for windless
day, but such air is rare.

This day moves along,
seasonal weather blowing
First, I work my paddle

against the flow, against
a wash of waves, against
a constant current,

against the wind-grain,
hiding as I can on lee
shore but on my return,

I change to paddle-sail,
a billowing blue circle
blown out and filled by air.

I set course for the return
after a haul heading up-wind
to mid-stream for full blow,

a burly Beauford four or more.
I hold white braided jib line
and set my stern to the wind

to enjoy a slick free ride
courtesy of this wild wind.
My kayak, now a convertible,

top-down and full speed
the wind blowing through my hair
down-hill all the way home!

## Otter Apropos

Otter curled over the breaking wake
of a fast Mercury-propelled ski boat
ignoring the noisy eruption of a gas
guzzling, noisy din & vibrating assault
on pristine could-have-been quiet.

As the first people learned adaptations
paddling within quiet dug-out canoes
fishing in treaty waters, these cohabitating
otters also shared the fishing abundance
through the seasons of ice and wild rice.

While otter families too have moved further
away far into the windswept back bays,
they remain true to their natural gifts
as playful pups now rolling over wave curl
and diving under knives of sharp-edged props.

# Bear vs Paddle

Black bear
rustling through tall
wetland grass
heard before seen
arrives at water's edge
of Four-mile Creek.
Moderate current
pushed lone kayak,
no shore bank to stop,
just more tall reeds.
My paddle seemed
a mere toothpick
without spear tip—
made for pushing,
not for beating,
yet bear lumbered
on into water, black
boulder-sized head
bobbed along, eyes
intent on opposite
grassy green bank—
as oblivious of kayak
as the running river
currently moving along.

# Embraced

After long, hot kayak,
I shove ashore and
abandon paddle to
embrace my mother.

Water flushes my hot
face, pulls the heat
from my tired body,
caresses me as a baby.

I go to mother who
supports and engulfs
me as before my birth,
every hair washed

and flesh licked clean.
Like the otter and beaver
I must surface for air
buoyant in mother's arms,

I swim with my cousins—
my kayak ashore, afloat.

# Breath of Decay

What need has eternity
for time?

Yet seeds are not timed,
frozen centuries—
some slide into the mud,
spring soup, then regenerate—

time reinvested too,
now as measure of death
on scale of decay
of a new green life

arising to decay
spending energy
sending echoing rings
timed to the beat of

a heart, length
of a breath.

# Wildly Away

Predator vs prey is the wild order of this
wilderness world where wolf and bear
rule the forest, osprey and eagle the river.

Prey adapts, produces offspring prodigiously.
Rabbit and field mouse use summer warm
to oven so many litters, hiding, camouflaged.
Rabbits run zig-zagging, not straight away.

Yet predator vs. predator is a full-out war
for staking out survival territory, preserving
prey for strongest and fittest, food for young.

A bald eagle dared soar too close to an osprey nest;
two dive-bomb, swooping from sky bearing down
on eagle who abandons fresh fish to get away

wildly away lest predator is prey!

# Plastic Clouds

Walk shore's last strewn-line
just beyond waves pushing jetsam
and flotsam ashore to find drift-
wood and roots, white fish bones,

many feathers of gulls and shore
birds, all nature's debris. Rounded
pebbles and stones also churn up

and wash ashore, never sharp-edged
as if chiseled off a sheer rock face,
wave action against grinding sand
for thousands of years rounded them.

Soft wispy cirrus clouds lace a pale
blue sky always flowing with music
except for an unnatural fine white line,
a contrail interrupting lacy delicacy

much as plastic water bottles, old lids,
monofilament fishing lines, and rubber
condoms assault a natural shoreline

with the insults of our ugliest din awash
at the edge of nature's high-water mark.

# Kayaking the Moon

I've given up full-throated howling at the moon,
and Hubby and I have surrendered our yearly
celebration sipping some honey under the moon.

I'm long past the days my body flooded
with phases of the moon tide, half-crazed
and shunned by men oblivious to our cycles.

I've given up riding rollercoasters at night,
dipping up and down, screaming on joy rides
followed by quiet moon time in the tunnel of love.

Yet still, I kayak in the slipstream of a full moon,
flashlight-free hands able to pull my paddle
inside this moonbeam to the end of the line,

the end of a skyline, a lifeline, a byline.

# Vespers

recited under
gray clouds following
a rainy, dark day

earlier, rising at dawn
under a canopy of clouds
a curtain opened—

sun slipped through
the slit of cloud and horizon
as a blood-red dawn

filled whole sky in risen
red reflecting under
an expansive cloud canopy

with whole horizon
drenched in solar color
as if living on Red Planet.

At mid-day, the outlook
still glowed, though dank,
since rising with red

drenched the soul
in crimson joy and song.
No dull day can defuse

such a brightening
rinse. Sleeper may embrace
this gray blanket tonight.

# Stages of Life

First, I paddled an Eddyline Sea Star blue and white
sleek, seventeen-foot kayak with a teak centerboard
down the keel keeping this long slender craft from
yawing, I soon became the fastest paddler on the flowage
as if coming in first somewhere still meant something.

When my life's partner finally gave up his fast gas toys
he became attracted to my pure pursuit of sitting
flat on the very top of the water's surface. Bagged Klepper
Aurius, a two-person kayak, became our passion,
a folding kayak made with precision only German's
could muster with wooden frame and collapsing
centerboard that enveloped front and back into
a canvas sleeve with a rubberized hull, fully portable.

We could access water anywhere, so even Louis
and Clarke could have wished for such a craft carried
into backwaters and outback, unexplored bodies—
wetlands, wilderness waters or streams with currents
running over sandbars, nothing stopped us. It also had a sail
with attaching outriggers. We soon became uninhibited
in finding habitats almost anywhere fit for the intrepid.

Older now, my last kayak is single fourteen-foot Kestrel
built by Current Designs with a comfy wide beam for
easy in-out. It is an age-appropriate craft keeping me
afloat. My partner has one of his own and paddles
point A to point B as is his aim; I find the back streams
through shallow wetlands opening into wide ponds.
I meditate on teeming life coming to reproduce out
of the torrents and fast life. Turtles, sometimes eight
or more, lay atop long logs sunning while I drift along.

# Campfire

We sit lakeside
on solid earth
watch our ring of fire
consume pine tree limbs—

sitting upwind breathe-in
pine soaked air,
watch as stars intermingle
with dancing sparks

exploding from sap
pockets, boil-bursting
in licking flames:
Earth, Air, Fire, Water,

elements of creation.
We pay quiet homage
just as cave-dwelling
ancestors once did

with same fire under same stars.

# The Great Spirit Soars

I sit atop the tall Great Totem,
white feathers, windswept,

sit atop earth's full life cycle,
all others prey within kingdom.

I take flight to great blue sky
soaring over rivers reaching,

extend my wide dark wings
finding drafts heaving off cliffs.

I settle my nest in the tallest pine
so hatchlings will know their place,

descend from the clouds, sharp
yellow eyes focused on river trout.

I descend to my abundant kingdom
far below my woody nest to know

the depths of these great heights,
for I am the Great Spirit. I Soar.

# Skimming the Surface

Paddling within my kayak
in rhythm with wind and waves
breath and heartbeat—

focusing thoughts on the river,
a stream of consciousness
current to this instant—

losing this consciousness
just brain-stem action
blending colors of river prism

muscle memory pulling
core force of this kayak
balancing the limited and endless flow

in rhythm with a ribbon of river
and mystic muse of the watery world—
only skimming the surface.

# Finishing the Silence

What is more rare than a blue sky
                without a solitary white cloud?

What is more fleeting than a crimson sunset
                under such sky?

What is more peaceful than the absence of wind
                to upset this last light?

What is quieter than a great body of water
                resting at total calm?

Where else a sandy shore gently embraced
                by caressing wavelets.

Where else must we stop our breath
                to finish this deep silence.

Where else, our only response a thankful prayer.

# About the Author

Patricia Carney lives in Cudahy, Wisconsin, along the south shore of Lake Michigan, English Major at U. of Wisconsin—Milwaukee, and received a Juris Doctorate at Marquette University, member of the Wisconsin Fellowship of Poets and South Shore Poets; her poems have appeared widely throughout the mid-west region along with numerous anthologies including most recently in Bramble (Summer 2020), lit. magazine of WFOP, and first-place winner in a juried ekphrastic poetry competition at Inspiration Studios, February 2020.; author of two chapbooks, BIRDBRAINS, 2016, in cooperation with a member of the Audubon Society in celebration of birding and To the MUS(sic), 2018, and novel, COMMUNITY SERVICE ON PLANET WEIRDO, 2019;

Her love of kayaking brought her each July, along with her extended family, spending the premier month of summer, to the northern woods of Wisconsin to kayak and explore the Turtle-Flambeau Flowage. Each trip is a spiritual journey into a unique river ecosystem first depicted on a carved totem pole that sits along the shores of the flowage. Documenting trips on a spiral memo pad with iPhone pics, these adventures flowed into the poems of this collection.

Located in Iron County in Northern Wisconsin, the Turtle-Flambeau Flowage was created in 1926 by the construction of a dam to create a reservoir and harness the power from the confluence of two rivers, creating 114 miles of winding flowage shoreline amid 195 islands, totaling nearly 19,000 acres of sparkling waterway. While the dam was originally controversial, the Wisconsin Stewardship Program preserved nearly 95% of the shoreline, which is now protected within a State Conservancy. WI DNR now calls the flowage the "crown jewel of the north." Kayakers often compare the Turtle-Flambeau to the Boundary Waters of Lake Superior in Minnesota because of its pristine wilderness. Carney has kayaked these waters for over 25 years.